Genius or Madman?

Sir Isaac Newton

Library of Congress Cataloging-in-Publication Data

Atkinson, Mary, 1966-
   Genius or madman? : Sir Isaac Newton / by Mary Atkinson.
      p. cm.
   Includes index.
   ISBN-10: 0-531-17770-X (lib. bdg)
   ISBN-13: 978-0-531-17770-9 (lib. bdg)
   ISBN-10: 0-531-18840-X (pbk)
   ISBN-13: 978-0-531-18840-8 (pbk)
   1. Newton, Isaac, Sir, 1642-1727. 2. Physicists--Great Britain--Biography. I. Title.

   QC16.N7A83 2008
   530'.092--dc22
   [B]

2007012403

Published in 2008 by Children's Press, an imprint of Scholastic Inc.,
557 Broadway, New York, New York 10012
www.scholastic.com

08 09 10 11 12 13 14 15 16 17
10 9 8 7 6 5 4 3 2 1

Printed in China through Colorcraft Ltd., Hong Kong

Author: Mary Atkinson
Educational Consultant: Ian Morrison
Editor: Mary Atkinson
Illustrator: Spike Wademan
Designer: Pirzad Rustomjee
Photo Researcher: Jamshed Mistry

Photographs by: Big Stock Photo (p. 5); **Getty Images** (cover; portrait of Newton, p. 11; Vincent
van Gogh, p. 30); **©Jason Massey/www.photographersdirect.com** (Grantham today, p. 15);
Jennifer and Brian Lupton (teenagers, pp. 32–33); **Photolibrary** (p. 7; Newton's birthplace,
p. 11; apothecary, p. 13; prism experiment, pp. 16–17; Newton and apple, pp. 18–19; pp. 22–23;
John Flamsteed, p. 25; p. 27; Einstein outdoors, pp. 28–29; George Washington Carver, p. 30);
Popperfoto (statue unveiling, p. 15); **Stock X.chng** (p. 34); **The Governors of The King's School,
Grantham, Lincolnshire** (King's School, p. 13); **Tranz: Corbis** (cover; p. 3; pp. 8–9; Aristotle,
Cambridge University, p. 17; woodcut, p. 19; pp. 20–21; *Principia Mathematica*, p. 25;
Einstein as a child, lecturing, p. 29; p. 31; student, pp. 32–33)

The publisher would like to thank Sue Long of King's School, Grantham, for the photograph
of the school on page 13.

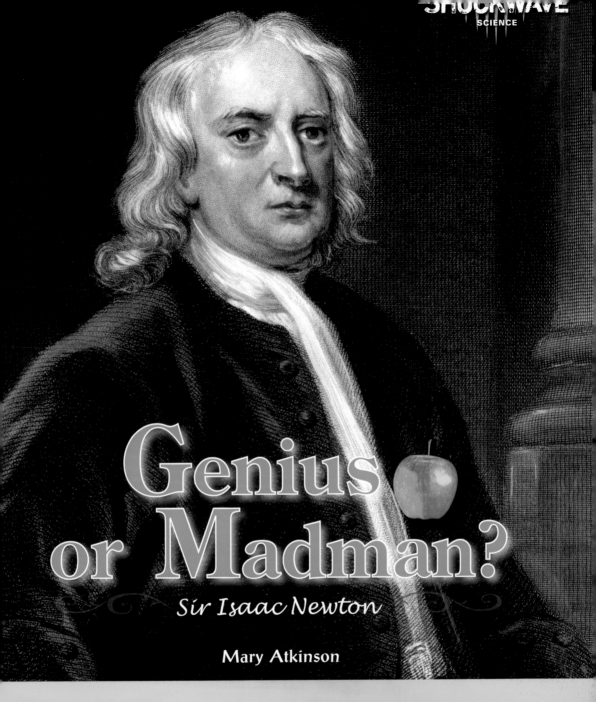

Genius or Madman?

Sir Isaac Newton

Mary Atkinson

children's press®

An imprint of Scholastic Inc.
NEW YORK • TORONTO • LONDON • AUCKLAND • SYDNEY
MEXICO CITY • NEW DELHI • HONG KONG
DANBURY, CONNECTICUT

CHECK THESE OUT!

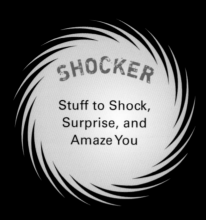

SHOCKER

Stuff to Shock,
Surprise, and
Amaze You

Quick Recaps
and Notable
Notes

Word Stunners
and Other Oddities

The Heads-Up
on Expert Reading

Links to More
Information

CONTENTS

apothecary (*uh POTH uh kair ee*) someone who makes and sells medicines; a pharmacist

calculation the use of math to determine a solution

experiment a test that a scientist does to figure out what will happen in a particular situation

genius (*GEE nyuss*) someone with extraordinary talents or intelligence, especially in some specific field of study, such as math, science, music, or art

gravity the force that pulls objects toward the center of the earth

mass the amount of matter of which something is made up

obsessed having such an extreme interest in something that little else is thought about

For additional vocabulary, see Glossary on page 34.

A number of words are related to the word *calculation*. These include *calculated, calculating,* and *calculator*. A kind of math invented by Newton himself is called *calculus*.

Sir Isaac Newton is one of the most famous scientists of all time. Although he died about 280 years ago, most of the **calculations** scientists use today are based on his discoveries. Newton was so clever that most people consider him a **genius**.

Many writers of the past depicted Newton as perfect in every way. They treated him like a storybook hero. However, we now know that these characterizations of Newton were far from accurate.

Like many very intelligent people, Newton did much of his important work while he was still a young man. He solved some of the biggest mysteries of science, and then had time left over for other things. One of his main interests was illegal at that time. His calculations and **experiments** were done in secret. They may even have driven him mad!

GREAT
BRITAIN

EUROPE

Grantham
Woolsthorpe Manor

ENGLAND

London

Newton lived in England,
which is part of Great Britain.

No Family Favorite

Isaac Newton always thought that he was important. He was born on December 25, 1642. It was Christmas Day. In England at that time, most people thought that it was a good sign to be born on this important Christian festival. However, Newton probably had a hard childhood. His father had died before Newton was born. When Newton was three, his mother remarried. She went to live with her new husband and left Newton with her parents. Newton's home was far from any town, and he would not have been allowed to play with many of the children living nearby. His family were landowners. In those days, landowners did not socialize with farmworkers. Interaction between people of different classes was restricted. Newton was probably lonely.

If Newton's father had lived, Newton may have never gone to school. Neither Newton's father nor his father's father had learned to read or write. It was Newton's grandparents on his mother's side of the family who decided to send him to school. The men in his mother's family were well educated. Newton's Uncle William had even attended university.

Newton's family home still stands. It is called Woolsthorpe Manor, although it is actually an ordinary-sized house. It is in Lincolnshire (*LING kin shuh*), England, and is open to visitors.

Facts
- born Dec. 25, 1642
- father died before Newton's birth
- lived away from any towns

Assumptions
- not allowed to play with many children
- Newton was lonely
- would not have gone to school if his father had lived

This is a portrait of Newton as a teenager. His long hair and large collar were the height of fashion for young men in the mid-1600s.

SCHOOL DAZE

At age twelve, Newton left home to attend school. At first, he showed few signs of being a genius. In those days, students were ranked to show their position in class. One year, Newton was ranked 78 out of 80. He was third from last! He also had few friends.

At Newton's school, students learned four main subjects: Latin, Greek, Bible studies, and math. Latin was the language spoken in the old Roman Empire. In Newton's time, it was the language used by scientists and other educated people. It allowed them to understand each other no matter which country they came from. Unfortunately, it also meant that people who hadn't learned Latin couldn't read important books.

SHOCKER

Graffiti was already a problem back in Newton's day. However, his old school is proud of a piece of stone in which Newton carved his name.

?

The word *daze* in the heading means "confused." In this case, it is also a play on the word *days*. From this heading, I can guess that Newton found his school days difficult.

While at school, Newton lived with the Clarkes, a local family. Mr. Clarke was an **apothecary**, and Newton may have learned about chemicals from him. As an adult, Newton used many chemicals in his experiments. As a schoolboy, however, he spent his free time making things out of wood. He invented all kinds of things, including a four-wheeled vehicle that he could sit in. It moved when he turned a handle.

Newton went to the King's School in the town of Grantham. It still stands, and it is still a school. However, students now study subjects such as computing and design technology.

In the 1600s, an apothecary's job was different from that of a modern-day **pharmacist**. An apothecary bought chemicals and mixed drugs by hand.

A FARMING FAILURE

Newton missed two years of school because his mother wanted him to run the family farm. She thought that he had learned enough. It was time he made himself useful. But Newton hated farming, and he was a terrible farmer. Instead of working, he spent his time reading and making mechanical models. Several times, he was fined for not noticing when his animals ate other farmers' crops.

Luckily for Newton, someone came to his rescue. Even though he was not at the top of his class, his old teacher, Mr. Stokes, had noticed how clever Newton was. Mr. Stokes contacted Newton's family. He said that Newton could live in the Stokes household for free if he went back to school. Newton's uncle told his mother she should accept the offer. Eventually, she agreed. Fear of having to spend his life as a farmer made Newton a better student. He worked hard so that he could go to a university.

Newton was lucky because:

- his old teacher had noticed that he was clever
- he was given an opportunity to go back to school
- he was offered free accommodation
- his family agreed to let him take up the offer

Newton lived with his teacher in the town of Grantham (above) so that he could attend school. The town was seven miles from his family farm. In the days before cars, this distance was too far for a student to travel every day.

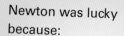

One night, young Newton gave the people of Grantham a fright. As part of an experiment, he flew a kite with a lantern attached to it. Those who saw the low-flying light had no idea what it was.

In 1858, the town of Grantham honored Newton by erecting a statue of him. A large crowd turned up for the statue's unveiling.

CAMBRIDGE BLUES

At age eighteen, Newton went to Cambridge (*CAME bridge*) University. Back then, many boys went to college at age fourteen. (Girls were not allowed to go at all!) Newton was older than most new students because he had missed so much school when he was farming.

Newton's mother had an **income** of £700 (**pounds**) a year, which is equivalent to about $100,000 today. However, she gave Newton only £10 a year for college. To pay his way, he worked as a servant for a senior member of the university. Luckily, the man was hardly ever at Cambridge. Most of the time, Newton was free to do as he pleased.

SHOCKER

In Newton's time, students who did badly in their final exams sometimes paid the examiner money to give them a passing grade. Newton had to give his examiner money, and even then, he just barely passed!

In those days, neither the students nor the teachers did much work. Newton was soon bored. Instead of doing the work that was assigned to him, he studied what interested him. Although his grades were poor, people started to notice how smart he was.

Newton did experiments to test his ideas. When experimenting with a **prism**, he became the first person to realize that light is made up of all the colors in the rainbow.

In the 1600s, most university students studied the works of Aristotle (*AR is staht uhl*). Aristotle was a Greek **philosopher** who died in 322 B.C. However, Aristotle did not carry out many experiments to prove his ideas. Newton thought that ideas should be tested, not just accepted because they sounded right.

> *I am a friend of Aristotle, but truth is my greater friend.*
> *– Isaac Newton*

Today, Cambridge is one of the top universities in the world. The students, both women and men, must work much harder to pass than they did in Newton's time.

A TRUE GENIUS

Newton became **obsessed** with learning. While most other students were happy to study what their teachers already knew, Newton wanted to know more. He wanted to know what the greatest thinkers thought, and he wanted to expand on their ideas. In his first year at Cambridge, he learned all there was to know about math at that time. He also read the writings of Galileo, the scientist who made the first useful telescope.

When Newton was studying for his second degree, the **plague** struck England. Many people fled crowded towns, where the disease spread quickly from person to person. Cambridge was shut down, so Newton moved back to his family home. However, he kept on working. It was during this time that, one day, he noticed an apple fall from a tree. No one knows exactly what happened – even Newton himself told several different versions of the story. We do know, however, that the falling apple made him think that the force of **gravity** must extend up into the sky and out into space. It led him to think that even the moon might be affected by Earth's gravity.

> I wasn't sure what *obsessed* meant. Instead of looking up the definition first, I continued reading. I got the idea that it meant something like "being committed" or "being driven." Then I read the definition. I was right! Reading on often helps me understand new words.

We shall call it gravity from now on.
– **Isaac Newton**

SHOCKER
Newton is famous for the story of the falling apple. In some versions of the story, the apple hits Newton on the head. The less-exciting truth is that the apple fell near him.

This woodcut shows people fleeing the plague in the 1600s. The skeleton tells us that they took the plague with them, spreading it to other places.

Facts About Plague

- Plague is caused by a kind of bacteria. Bacteria are tiny living things that are too small to be seen without a microscope.

- Most plague victims catch the disease when they are bitten by fleas infected with the bacteria.

- Symptoms include fever, headache, weakness, swollen glands, and dark patches on the skin.

- Death can follow first symptoms within one day.

- In Newton's time, the plague affected the city of London particularly severely. More than 75,000 Londoners died.

- In the 1300s, plague killed as many as 30 million people in Europe. In the 1800s, it killed about 20 million people.

- Plague still exists. Today, it is treated with **antibiotic** medicines.

WHAT NEWTON KNEW

When Newton was still in his twenties, he came up with three of the most important scientific discoveries of all time. He could have become instantly famous, but he kept his ideas to himself. No one knows why he didn't publish them until about 20 years later. Some say he wanted to perfect them first. Others say he enjoyed keeping them secret. These are the things he discovered:

- He realized that the same force – gravity – keeps us on the ground and keeps the planets in **orbit** around the sun. At the same time, he described the three laws of motion (right).

- Newton invented a kind of math called calculus. Today, engineers and many scientists use calculus to figure out values that change with time.

- Newton did experiments to learn the nature of light and color. He showed that white light is made up of light of all the colors in the rainbow. He also invented a reflecting telescope that used mirrors instead of glass lenses. These kinds of telescopes are still used today.

Newton made his reflecting telescope himself. He even bought the metal to make his own mirror.

Newton's ideas were so new that the scientific words he needed to describe them didn't exist. He invented many scientific terms, such as **mass**, *gravity*, and *force*.

People can use marbles to experiment with Newton's laws of motion for themselves.

People already knew that Earth and the other planets orbited the sun. However, Newton explained for the first time why that is so.

Newton's Laws of Motion

1. An object moves in a straight line or stays at rest unless a force acts on it.

2. How much an object **accelerates** depends on its mass and how much force is applied to it.

3. Forces act in pairs. Every action has an equal and opposite reaction.

In Newton's time, new words were needed to describe new ideas. New words are still being created today, for example: *laptop*, *ethernet*, and *multitask*.

THE PHILOSOPHER'S STONE

Newton became so excited about his ideas that he often forgot
to eat. He would go to dinner but forget to look up from his book.
He also worked late into the night, getting very little sleep. He
seldom went out or got any exercise. Not surprisingly, people
found him unfriendly and grumpy. Perhaps he was unsociable
because he didn't want anyone to know what he was doing.

Much of Newton's time was spent searching for something
he would never find – the philosopher's stone. This
was a substance that people thought would turn
ordinary metals into gold. It was thought to bring
great wisdom to those who discovered it.
The science of the search was known as
alchemy (*AL kuh mee*). It was also illegal!

SHOCKER

Newton once pushed a needle
into his eye socket to see what
would happen if he changed
the shape of his eye. Another
time, he stared at the sun and
lost his sight for several days.
In both cases, he was very
lucky not to have blinded
himself permanently.

Newton had about 175 books on alchemy. He did many experiments. He also wrote detailed notes, often writing in code so that no one could steal his ideas. There is a story that he lost many of his notes when a dog knocked over a candle, setting them alight. However, no one is sure if this actually happened.

Newton once went to his study to get a book for a visitor and forgot what he was doing. He sat down and got on with his work.

… but the hidden secret modus is Clissus Paracelsi wch is nothing else but the separation of the principles thris purification & reunion in a fusible & penetrating fixity.

In 2005, some of Newton's lost notes on alchemy were discovered. They were in English, but they contained coded language. Newton had certainly succeeded in making them hard for others to understand!

NEWTON'S RIVALS

In 1687, Newton finally published his ideas on gravity and motion. The book was written in Latin, and it was known as *Principia Mathematica* (*Principles of Mathematics*). It made Newton famous. However, with fame came problems. Newton had never had many friends. Most people he knew were other scientists. Although he found it hard to get along with others, he also hated arguments. He especially hated people disagreeing with his ideas. One of his main rivals was scientist Robert Hooke. Hooke claimed to have discovered gravity before Newton, but he couldn't prove it. He also disagreed with Newton about his **theories** on light.

The word *principle* is a noun that means "a basic law or concept." The word *principal*, on the other hand, can be a noun meaning "the leader," or it can be an adjective meaning "most important."

Another rival was German mathematician Gottfried Leibniz. Like Newton, Leibniz invented calculus. He probably invented it after Newton, but he published the information first. Leibniz asked the Royal Society (the national science academy) to decide who was first. Unfortunately for Leibniz, Newton belonged to the Royal Society, and he chose the committee members investigating the case. They decided that Newton was first.

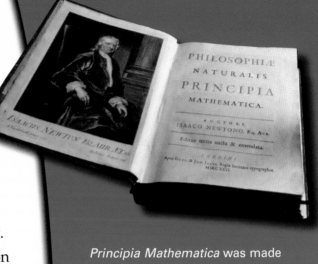

Principia Mathematica was made up of three volumes. It was very detailed, and it soon developed a reputation for being difficult to understand.

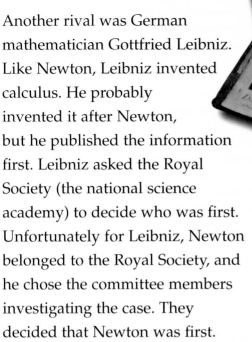

The astronomer John Flamsteed was yet another rival. Flamsteed felt that Newton treated him like a servant, not a fellow scientist. He wanted more respect from Newton.

BREAKDOWN

In 1693, Newton had a **nervous breakdown**. Historians have debated how serious it was and what caused it. Some say it was just a minor setback caused by his arguments with other scientists. Others say that it was caused by poisoning. Newton used poisonous chemicals, such as mercury and lead, in his experiments. These metals can cause mental-health problems, such as moodiness and memory loss. However, they probably weren't the main cause of his breakdown: Newton recovered. People do not recover from this kind of poisoning.

There is no doubt, though, that Newton had an unusual personality. He was antisocial, forgetful, obsessive, and very sensitive to criticism. Some of these things got worse as he grew older. Maybe this was because of poisoning. In his writings, he mentions tasting mercury. Recently, scientists tested a lock of his hair. As they suspected, it had a very high level of mercury.

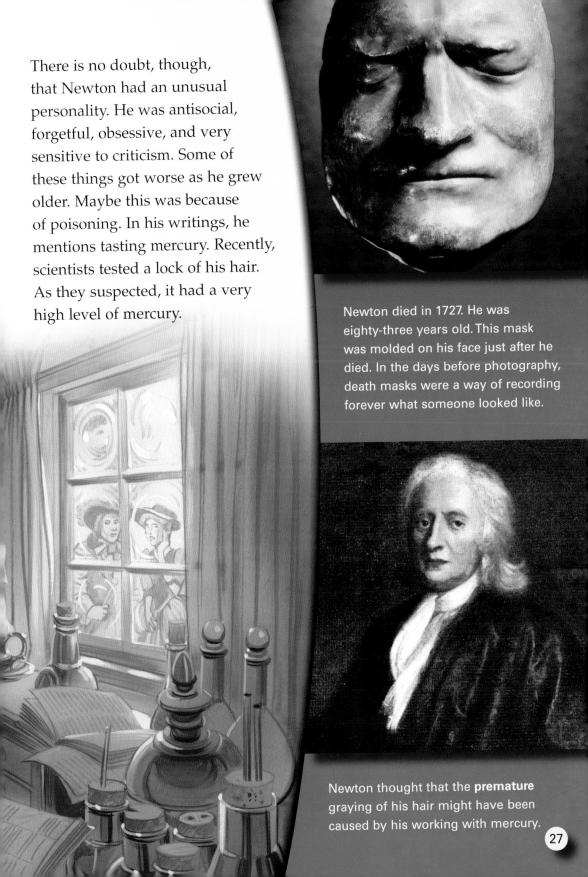

Newton died in 1727. He was eighty-three years old. This mask was molded on his face just after he died. In the days before photography, death masks were a way of recording forever what someone looked like.

Newton thought that the **premature** graying of his hair might have been caused by his working with mercury.

ANOTHER GENIUS

Newton was a **physics** genius. Even today, many of the calculations scientists use are based on Newton's work. However, in the early 1900s, scientists began noticing that there were instances when the classical physics of scientists such as Newton produced inaccurate results. This happened when scientists were measuring things that were very, very small or very, very fast.

The **physicist** Albert Einstein helped resolve these problems. He published groundbreaking papers that were so advanced that even today most people cannot understand them. For instance, he said that mass and energy can change into one another. He also said that gravity makes time go more slowly. Einstein's work on gravity gave scientists a much more accurate understanding of what gravity is. Just like Newton in his time, Einstein became instantly famous when he published his ideas. Even today, many people think of Einstein when they hear the word *genius*.

I've heard of Einstein. I remember this really clever kid that some people said was an Einstein. Now I understand why. That kid was really smart!

Like Newton, Einstein did poorly at college. He often missed classes so that he could instead study the physics books and journals that interested him.

As a child, Einstein (above right) was slow to talk. His parents were worried. Of course, they had no idea that he would become known as one of the greatest thinkers of all time.

In his old age, Einstein had a shock of scruffy, white hair and a wide mustache. This look came to be a symbol for scientific genius. However, at the time when Einstein came up with his great theories, he was still a young man with tidy, dark hair.

Einstein's general theory of relativity says that $E = mc^2$, but what does that mean? It tells us that the amount of energy (E) contained in something equals its mass (m) times the speed of light (c) times the speed of light again. C is a huge number (186,282 miles per second), so the equation tells us that even tiny amounts of matter contain enormous amounts of energy.

REMARKABLE MINDS

There is a big difference between being intelligent and being a genius. While many people are smart in one or more ways, few people are geniuses. Most people considered to be geniuses have shown exceptional originality. However, being a genius certainly does not guarantee an easy life. Many remarkable thinkers have had hard lives. In some cases, this was due to poverty or prejudice. Others have had mental-health problems. Some scientists think that in some cases there may be a link between genius and mental illness.

George Washington Carver (1864–1943)
Although born a slave, Carver grew up to become a scientist who improved the lives of many farmers in the American South. His crop rotation systems made farms more productive. He also invented more than 400 products made from either peanuts or sweet potatoes.

Vincent van Gogh (1853–1890)
Vincent van Gogh was a Dutch artist. Today, his paintings are worth a fortune. However, he made very little money during his lifetime. He also suffered from **depression**, and at one stage, he cut off his own earlobe.

Virginia Woolf (1882–1941)

Virginia Woolf was a gifted English writer. She wrote in a very experimental way. She explored her characters' emotions and personalities with great creativity. Her novels are still read and studied by university students today. Woolf had several nervous breakdowns, the first when she was still a teenager. At age fifty-nine, she felt she was going insane and drowned herself.

Marie Curie (1867–1934)

Marie Curie was a brilliant physicist. She was born in Poland, but lived in France as an adult. Curie won two Nobel Prizes for her discoveries about the nature of radiation. Curie died of cancer at age sixty-seven. It was probably caused by contact with radiation during her experiments.

Name	Field	Accomplishment
van Gogh	art	spectacular paintings
Carver	science	crop-rotation systems
Curie	science	nature of radiation
Woolf	literature	experimental writing

Neither Newton nor Einstein did well at college. Instead of attending classes or studying what they were told to study, they read books about physics. They were not lazy – they worked hard. They also knew more about physics than most of the other students! Today, they are remembered as two of the greatest scientific minds of all time.

WHAT DO YOU THINK?

Should students who are especially adept at one particular subject be allowed to study what they want to study rather than learn with a class group?

PRO

We should make it easy for future geniuses to work. That way, they will make more progress, and we will all benefit from their discoveries. I think it is important that all kids get to learn in the best environment for them.

Some people believe that students should attend schools where they can study subjects that interest them, and do so independently or at a level that suits them. Otherwise, they may become bored and unruly in class. Others think that all students should be exposed to the same curriculum and simply learn at their own pace, without special classes.

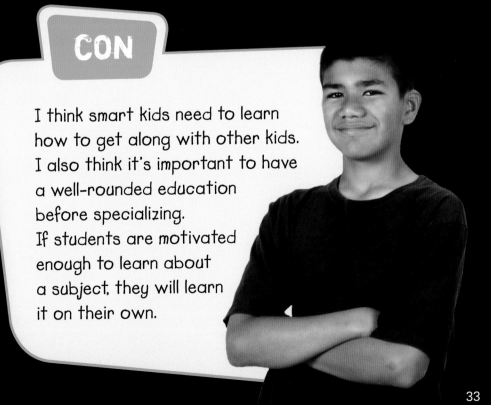

CON

I think smart kids need to learn how to get along with other kids. I also think it's important to have a well-rounded education before specializing. If students are motivated enough to learn about a subject, they will learn it on their own.

GLOSSARY

accelerate to gain speed

antibiotic (*an ti bye OT ik*) a drug, such as penicillin, that kills bacteria and is used to fight disease

depression a mental illness characterized by low spirits, low energy, and difficulty with concentration

income the money that someone earns or is given

nervous breakdown a mental-health event in which a person is unable to cope emotionally or mentally

orbit to move in a regular path around something, especially a planet, the sun, or another heavenly body

pharmacist a person who sells medicines. Modern pharmacists often work in drugstores.

philosopher (*fih LOSS uh fer*) a person who studies truth, wisdom, and the nature of reality

physicist (*FIZ uh sist*) someone who studies physics, which is the science of matter and energy

physics (*FIZ iks*) the study of matter and energy

plague (*PLAYG*) a very contagious disease caused by bacteria

pound the currency used in Britain. A pound is similar to a dollar.

premature early; happening before it is expected to happen

prism a see-through solid object with flat sides

theory an idea about why something happens

Pound notes

FIND OUT MORE

BOOKS

Delano, Marfe Ferguson. *Genius: A Photobiography of Albert Einstein.*
National Geographic Society, 2005.

Krull, Kathleen. *Isaac Newton.* Viking, 2006.

MacLeod, Elizabeth. *George Washington Carver: An Innovative Life.*
Kids Can Press, 2007.

Oxlade, Chris. *Gravity.* Heinemann Library, 2006.

Parker, Steve. *Marie Curie and Radium.* Chelsea House Publishers, 1995.

WEB SITES

Go to the Web sites below
to learn more about
the scientists in this book.

www.newton.cam.ac.uk/newtlife.html

www.projectshum.org/Gravity/

www.light-science.com/newtonapple.html

www.einstein-website.de/contentskids.html

www.nps.gov/archive/gwca/expanded/gwc.htm

www.hypatiamaze.org/curiforkids/curie_kids.html

INDEX

ABOUT THE AUTHOR

Mary Atkinson is the author of many fiction and nonfiction books for children. She also has a science degree. For the past eighteen years, she has worked as a writer and an editor. Mary hopes that this book will bring to life the story of a brilliant but troubled scientist who lived hundreds of years ago. She would like readers to discover that even the world's greatest thinkers had real problems and that they made many mistakes, just like the rest of us.